IMAGES
of America

APOPKA

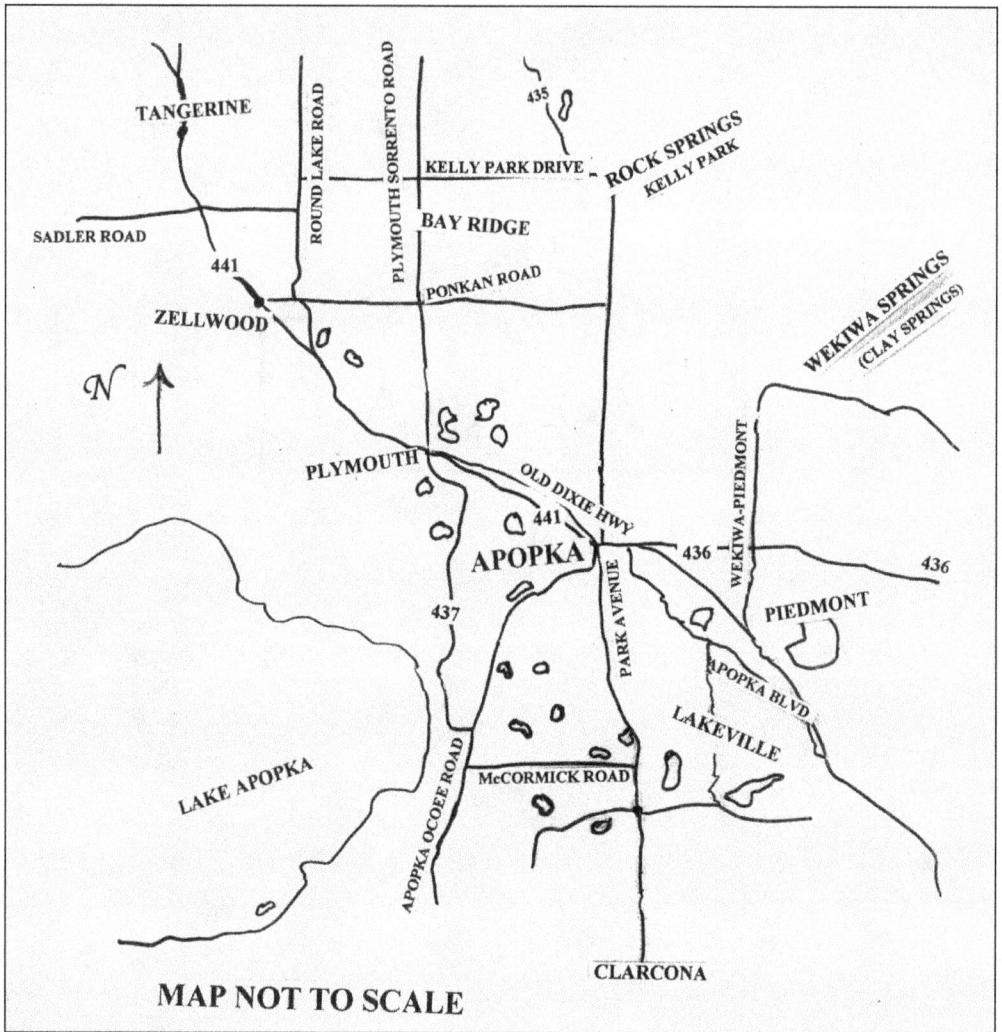

TANGERINE

ROUND LAKE ROAD

PLYMOUTH SORRENTO ROAD

435

KELLY PARK DRIVE

ROCK SPRINGS

KELLY PARK

SADLER ROAD

BAY RIDGE

441

PONKAN ROAD

WEKIWA SPRINGS

(CLAY SPRINGS)

ZELLWOOD

N ↑

PLYMOUTH

OLD DIXIE HWY

WEKIWA-PIEDMONT

441

APOPKA

436

436

437

PARK AVENUE

PIEDMONT

APOPKA BLVD

LAKEVILLE

APOPKA OCOEE ROAD

LAKE APOPKA

McCORMICK ROAD

CLARCONA

MAP NOT TO SCALE

The areas covered in this book are Apopka, Bay Ridge, Clarcona, Piedmont, Plymouth, Tangerine, and Wekiwa Springs, with special emphasis on Apopka.

IMAGES
of America

APOPKA

Apopka Historical Society Book Committee

ARCADIA
PUBLISHING

Published by Arcadia Publishing
Charleston, South Carolina

Library of Congress Catalog Card Number: 2003114612

For all general information contact Arcadia Publishing at:
Telephone 843-853-2070
Fax 843-853-0044
E-mail sales@arcadiapublishing.com
For customer service and orders:
Toll-Free 1-888-313-2665

Visit us on the Internet at www.arcadiapublishing.com

This postcard view of U.S. 441 in Apopka, Florida, facing east, was taken about 1931.

4

CONTENTS

ACKNOWLEDGMENTS

The book committee members gratefully acknowledge the enthusiasm people have shown in sharing their family histories. The Apopka Historical Society recognized the need for a book to present and preserve a sample pictorial history of Apopka, as so much history has been lost. Requests were issued by word of mouth, phone calls to members of the society, and the *Apopka Chief* newspaper for all to participate by sharing family photographs and memories. The following pages are the results of your efforts; without your contributions, this book would not be possible. All photographs and images are courtesy of the museum of the Apopkans, unless otherwise noted. Jerrell H. Shofner's book, *History of Apopka and Northwest Orange County, Florida*, has been quoted extensively in this document. His work is greatly appreciated. Please look, read, remember, and enjoy.

INTRODUCTION

With this book we will take you on a journey of the Apopka area's past. There will be glimpses of Bay Ridge, Clarcona, Piedmont, Plymouth, Zellwood, and Tangerine. These settlements share significantly in the shaping of Apopka and the northwest Orange County area.

There will be a view of people with their many diverse interests. They seized the opportunity to merge their cultures, along with their passions and hard work, to create Apopka, which has become the second largest city in Orange County in recent years. A long journey has elapsed since the Native Americans designated Apopka as "Big Potato!"

These pages bring to life such characters as Native Americans and early settlers—some from other states and some from other countries. The Pirie family enticed Northerners to select the Apopka area as their winter home. In later years the Pirie Estate was renamed Errol Estate, a golf course community. Another settlement, Piedmont, became the home of Swedish immigrants.

Citrus groves thrived on the Cohen Estate near Zellwood. Zellwood's name is the same as that given to a beautiful residence owned by Elwood Zell. The foliage, citrus, cattle industries, and vegetable-growing acreage on the Zellwood muck mark the determined efforts of early inhabitants who strived to turn their newly found sites into profitable ventures. One such venture was Plymouth Citrus Growers, which marketed, packaged, and shipped fresh citrus fruit across the country. Plymouth Citrus Products came along later as the producer of citrus by-products. Following World War II, Vacuum Foods, later to become Minute Maid Corporation, was located in Plymouth. "Fern City" once appeared on signs at city limits, touting Apopka's fern growing, but as the industry made strides in growth and propagation practices, that title took a back seat to the "Indoor Foliage Capital of the World."

You will see "The Lodge," which was the focal point of activities, including the central trading center for the area. The original building still stands today and has the distinction of being the oldest Masonic Lodge in the state of Florida, in continuous operation since 1859.

This book depicts setbacks endured by early Apopkans. The freezes and cyclones devastated their properties and caused untold hardships as they rebuilt their lives. These photographs reveal the progress made by these families, generation after generation.

Nature bestowed a beautiful pristine site with water emerging from a huge rock, thus the name, "Rock Springs." Dr. Howard A. Kelly, who owned the spectacular property, donated it to Orange County. Nearby Wekiwa Springs has the same type of pure water; both locations offer swimming and boating. Both sites have become well-maintained parks by both Orange County and the State of Florida.

Look closely at the group who joined together to build various structures, such as the William Edwards Hotel, which served the entire area upon its completion. Take pride with us as you see the progress made in every aspect of the early settlers' lives and their accomplishments. We show

how schools progressed and how parents were determined to have their children educated, even when children were sent to various churches for their daily studies when a cyclone demolished an early school. Note how students were transported in their horse–drawn school bus by teacher Miss Mattie Chapman. See the progress of school buildings and the growth in student bodies at each school.

Our journey will include pictures taken during World War II, showing some of the service men who fought and died for our freedoms.

Our photo journey brings in the various leaders of the area—those courageous men and women who never faltered in their determination to build a firm foundation for future generations. The city of Apopka has been led by Mayor John H. Land for more than 50 years at the writing of this journal. No other city in the state of Florida can equal such a distinction. Civic organizations—Rotary Club, Sertoma, the Elks Club, the Apopka Woman's Club, the Veterans of Foreign Wars—all return their energies to the community and beyond, with outreaches to many in need. The Foliage Festival, sponsored by the Woman's Club, has run annually for more than 42 years.

Religious services were important to settlers. Most of Apopka's churches represent generations of spiritual outreach to the community, serving a number of various cultures. There are currently over 90 churches in the area.

As we move along, you will note the continuing community interest in baseball, football, basketball, and tennis. History records Apopka's baseball fervor as its men played in the Lake Orange League. Apopka's Little League team went all the way to the top and returned home as national champions. Another honor was acclaimed with great pride when the Apopka Blue Darters captured the state football championship. The Pop Warner football championship was yet another claim to fame. There was a time when business firms closed their doors on Wednesday afternoons so storekeepers could join the many who faithfully attended the games each week. While into sports, some will remember the well-known Sportsmen's Club, which was founded by a group of men who maintained exclusive hunting sites in the Wekiwa Springs area. Lake Apopka, the second largest lake in Florida, was the mecca for many tourists who made annual trips to "Fisherman's Paradise" on its shores when it offered prime bass fishing.

It is with a deep sense of pride that we acknowledge those individual Apopkans who achieved recognition as professionals, bringing national attention to themselves and to their hometown area. Professional football player Warren Sapp even has a street named for him in Plymouth. Some will recall how John Anderson was seldom seen without his guitar as he grew up and that practicing brought him fame in the musical industry, especially with the song "Swingin'." A few years later, the group Sawyer Brown included local musicians Mark Miller and Greg Hubbard.

As we journey forward, we recognize that Walt Disney World caused this once sleepy bedroom community to evolve into a whole new concept of living. More people, more subdivisions, more cars, more roads, and more activities brought about extreme changes in many facets of daily life in the Apopka area.

And, now the journey into Apopka's history begins . . .

One

THE JOURNEY BEGINS
1845–1900

The Masonic Lodge #36 F & A.M., known as "The Lodge," was literally the center of the town—the city limits were established as one mile north, east, south, and west of the lodge. The lodge was built in 1859 of timbers assembled without nails. One corner of the building was supported by the stump of a pine tree felled during the clearing of the land. The lodge room was above the unfinished lower floor that served as a church, a school, and a store. It has the distinction of being the only lodge in Florida in continuous operation since 1859, except two years during the War between the States. The first floor was replaced by a concrete foundation and ground floor in 1952. The top floor was lowered and secured onto the new foundation and first floor.

Coacoochee, (Wild Cat.)

Coacoochee, or Wildcat, one of the most famous and influential war chiefs of the Second Seminole War, was born at Ahapopka. Coacoochee was living in Ahapopka as chief of a band of about 200 Native Americans and several African Americans when the Second Seminole War broke out in December of 1835. (Courtesy Anthropological Archives, Smithsonian Institute.)

Pictured here is a portion of a dugout canoe found in Plymouth, Florida, by landowner Charles Grinnell. It is displayed in the Museum of Apopkans. The canoe and the artifacts shown below bear witness to the Native American histories of Lake Apopka.

Artifacts have been unearthed on the shores of Lake Apopka and nearby muck lands in Zellwood, Plymouth, and Rock Springs. Art Dreaves has contributed many finds to the museum.

11

Peter, Thomas, and Joseph Buchan were all living in the Apopka area in 1854. Joseph and Peter Buchan served consecutively as justices of the peace from 1857 through 1866. Pictured here is Peter Buchan, who served as Worshipful Master of the Lodge from 1859 through 1866. Other early settlers included L.H. Clay, William S. Delk, W.G. Foote, and Samuel Stewart. Also found on the 1855 tax rolls are Philemon Bryan, James R. Stewart, and W.C. Goolsby.

In July of 1843 John L. Stewart and his two sons, Jonathan and Matthew, received permits for homesteads west of Lake Apopka under the authority of the Armed Occupation Act. The picture below, taken recently, shows Bettie Stewart Hicks in front of the old Stewart homestead in Plymouth.

Robert Barnhart operated a mill on the Upper Wekiwa River around 1854. The masonic lodge meetings were held at his mill until the lodge was built in 1859. He contracted to build the lodge, but his mill broke down. He served on the petit jury in 1857.

The First Baptist Church was organized in 1860 with Rev. George Powell as minister. The church was located on the northwest corner of the Old Church Cemetery, north of the Greenwood entrance.

Nicholas W. Prince moved his family from Alabama to Apopka in 1867. He served on the school board in 1870 and taught school in 1871. He was county superintendent of schools in 1872 and 1873. Pictured here is his daughter Mary Eliza Prince Hiers, who taught at the lodge in 1872 and 1873 and at Piedmont from 1889 to 1902. Her daughters Gertrude, Chattye, and Loula also taught in Apopka schools.

W.A. Lovell was superintendent of schools in 1869. He and his son operated a dry goods store and had many acres of citrus. He served on the building committee of the First Baptist Church of Apopka. W.A. Lovell and others incorporated the Orange County Central Telegraph Company in 1880 by building a line from Apopka, through Zellwood, to Lake Eustis.

14

Johan J. Anderson arrived in Piedmont from Sweden in 1870. He applied for citizenship in 1900. He married Rosa Hotz on Easter Sunday, April 7, 1901, in the schoolhouse-church in Piedmont. A copy of his citizenship application and their marriage license is on file at the Museum of Apopkans.

The Methodist Church was founded in 1870. Its first services were held in a schoolhouse on South McGee Avenue. When the church became uninhabitable in 1916 and funds were scarce, the Presbyterians offered to share their church. The First Methodist Church was built on the corner of Third Street and Park Avenue in 1922. On opening day at the new church, the Methodists assembled with the Presbyterians, and together they marched to the new Methodist church.

Dr. Zelotes Mason arrived in the area about 1871. He was a physician, a citrus grower, and an ardent supporter of Apopka, and he was involved in the development of the town. He was one of the 26 men who secured the town's charter. In 1883, he was Grand Master of the Masons of Florida. Also, he donated the property for the cemetery and was the first one to be buried there.

The First Presbyterian Church of Apopka was organized in 1873 by Zelotes Mason and J.M. Auld, ruling elders, and Reverend Wallace. This building, built in 1886, burned in 1951 and was rebuilt on the same site on Highland Street, facing east.

Frances Ann Lampp, born in 1856, and Wes Berry Raulerson, born in 1850, were married around 1873 in Palm Springs.

Mr. and Mrs. W.B. Raulerson moved to Apopka around 1873. They had ten children but only five lived to adulthood. Mr. Raulerson was a carpenter; he built many homes and barns, all with hand tools, in and around Apopka. His great-grandson Delbert Raulerson owns Raulerson's Nursery on Welch Road in Apopka with his wife, Carol.

Pictured is a Fourth of July picnic at Blue Lake in Piedmont, Florida, with members of the Olsen, Hotz, Larsson, Jackson, Anderson, Hanson, and Thollander families. The Swedish community built a dam, called "the box," to provide water for the winery that Jonas Larsson and Gust Jackson operated.

Charles F. Hiers came to Apopka in 1874. He was a merchant from 1874 to 1877, and was postmaster from March 1875 to December 1877. He married Mary Eliza Prince in March 1875.

Olaf Larsson arrived with his wife and two sons, Lars and Jonas, in December 1877, and settled in the Piedmont area. Jonas went to California to seek his fortune but returned in the late 1880s. Shown on the Piedmont property in 1895 are Lars and Olaf Larsson, Mrs. Lars Larsson, Olga Larsson, Mr. ? Yeager and other unidentified people. Many items from this family are on display at the Museum of the Apopkans.

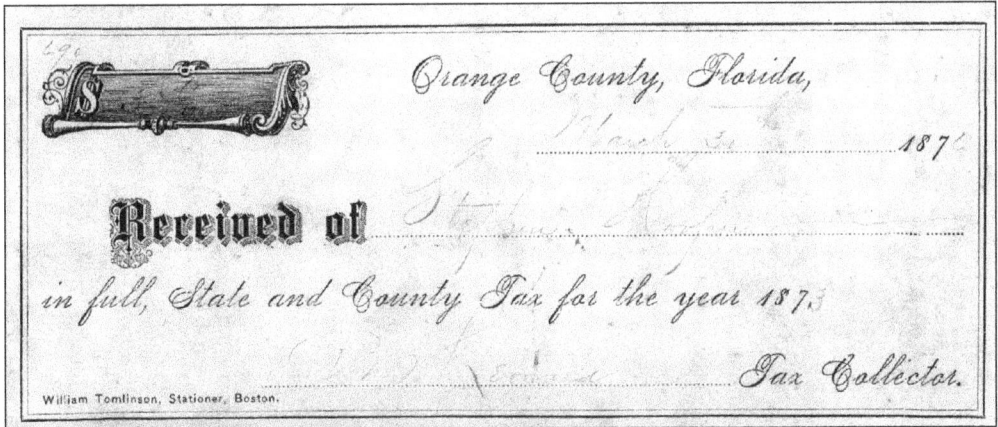

Stephen Hooper bought and sold land in 1876, as indicated by this tax receipt.

Hannah and August "Gust" Jackson provided the supper after the traditional Christmas party at the Piedmont school at their home. He served on the board of trade, was an early bus driver, co-owned the Piedmont winery, and owned the general merchandise store.

The centers of the Piedmont community were a small store operated by Gus Jackson and the schoolhouse-church, pictured below, which served as the social center.

E.J. Ryan came to Apopka in 1880 at the age of 13. In 1920, he began his lumber company, which became a family enterprise operating to the present day. He is shown here with his two sons, Mark and Nat Ryan, in the hardware store.

The Prince family built this 14-room house in the 1880s, and it was converted to the Oak's Hotel in 1916. It changed hands frequently and was bought by the Bryants, whose daughter, Mrs. J.G. Coleman, ran it as an apartment house until 1963. It was demolished in 1966.

John Steinmetz came from Pennsylvania in 1882. He planted citrus groves, built a packing house, and, after the freezes of 1894–1895, built a skating rink, which served as a church on Sundays. Telephone service began in 1901 when Henry Witherington and John Steinmetz erected a line from Clay Springs to Apopka. Steinmetz made many improvements at Clay Springs and developed the first amusement park in the area. He organized and led the Wild Life League in 1921.

About three miles northeast of Zellwood, Bay Ridge developed quickly when a group of about 30 families, mostly from New England, moved in during 1885–1886. They grew fruits and vegetables, built cisterns, had a saw and shingle mill, and manufactured starch. Blanche Schopke, shown on right, is a descendant of Henry Schopke, who was the proprietor of a general store in 1890. He is buried in the Oak Hill Cemetery in Bay Ridge with his wife and other descendants.

Amos and Mary J. Starbird moved from Freeman, Maine, with five of their sons in 1885. The Starbird family is pictured above in Forest City. Amos and his sons, Adelbert, Austin, Edwin, and Percival, operated sawmills in Forest City, Wekiwa (Clay Springs), Rock Springs, Apopka, and Moffitt, Florida. The Apopka Mill became the Consumer's Lumber and Veneer in 1903 and was operated by the Starbirds until 1920, when it caught fire and burned.

The Congregational Church was built in 1886 and was located on the northwest corner of Park Avenue and Fourth Street, on land purchased from John T. Champneys. It was discontinued after the freezes of 1894–1895. The property was purchased by the Episcopal church in 1902 for $75.00. Christmas Eve services were held there for the community for many years. The building was moved to the southeast corner of Highland and Sixth Street in 1979.

Almost all settlers had a few head of cattle for family needs as well as for bartering and security for loans. Every cattleman had a mark or brand. David Stewart, H.H. Witherington, A.J. Lovell, Sam Stewart, and Lafayette Pike served as inspectors. Lafayette Pike and his sons were known for their watchfulness over their herds.

St. Paul's African Methodist Episcopal Church was established on Broad Street in Johnson Town in the 1880s. In 1890 it was dismantled and moved to Mead's Bottom. In 1920 it was moved again, to the corner of Park Avenue and Tenth Street.

This family portrait of Charles B. Linn of Atlanta, Georgia, his wife Ida Brown Linn, and children Carl B. and Ruth Ann, was taken about 1888 in Apopka. Mr. Charles B. Linn owned a dry goods store, cattle, and citrus groves in Apopka. His son, Carl B., was one of the officials who organized the Apopka Baseball Club.

Clay Springs had few residents in the time after the War between the States. Adam Waterman, J.M. Auld, B.F. Carpenter, S.B. Harrington, J.B. Jeffcoat, and his relatives lived there. "The Springs" continued to be a popular bathing and picnic spot. This picture shows some of the improvements made by John Steinmetz in the 1890s.

William Edwards arrived in Zellwood in 1889. He soon became a leader in the cattle industry, managing Errol and Laughlin Estates. He was a Mason and a director of the State Bank of Apopka in 1912, and he served on the Orange County School Board in 1915, represented Zellwood in 1917 on the Orange County Council for Defense, was president of the Apopka Board of Trade in 1921, and was president of State Bank of Apopka in 1921. Mr. Edwards was president of Plymouth Citrus Exchange for 20 years. The William Edwards Hotel was named for him in 1926. He died in 1934.

The John Pirie family brought many cultural changes to the community and provided job opportunities on their Errol Farm.

The John T. Pirie family, from Illinois, began spending winters in Plymouth in 1892. Mr. Pirie built a showplace estate, called Errol Farm, on which he raised registered livestock and grew corn and velvet beans. Pictured is the beautiful home in background and the family riding in carriage with elegant horses.

W.T. Berry Sr. went to work for the Tavares Orlando and Atlantic Railroad in 1890 and continued as station agent in Apopka for 38 years. He was also an orange grower. His orange groves survived the freezes of 1894–1895, and the next year the only shipment of oranges from Apopka was four boxes from his groves. His granddaughter, Jeanette Robinson, served in city government in Apopka. Shown here are W.T. Berry Jr. with his granddaughter Marcia King.

This photo, taken from the north side of Lake Marshall, shows the devastation of the citrus groves after the freezes of December 1894 and February 1895. Oil smudge pots were burned to blanket the area with smoke and heat, which proved inadequate. The effect of these freezes caused so much heartache and hardship, as Apopka's economy at that time was far from robust. The financial ruin was widespread since business commitments and mortgage payments could not be met. Many families were forced to leave the area to seek employment opportunities elsewhere.

Two

SETTLING IN
1901–1920

Dr. Zelotes Mason hailed the region as "The Invalid's Refuge" and cited such inducements as good accommodations and good business opportunities. This enticed other Northerners to visit the state. The automobile made travel easier and encouraged people to consider moving to a new area.

The Apopka Union School students, teachers, and parents enjoy a picnic at Clay Springs on April 2, 1902.

Faculty members for Apopka Union School in 1903–1904 were Misses Mary Dart, Lena Short, Lula Davis, and Emma Dart.

This 1904 photo shows the Apopka Union School, which was accredited by the State of Florida in 1901. Education was very important to the citizens of Apopka.

To improve their location, the Baptists bought property at Fourth and Highlands and built the new church pictured here in 1906.

This beautiful building was the Frank S. Witherby Grocery and Produce Store, located on Central Avenue. Clyde Love is in the buggy, and Mr. Witherby is standing by the water pump.

In 1906, Consumers Lumber and Veneer employed about 100 people and contributed greatly to the economic stability of the community.

The Consumers Lumber and Veneer tram operated between the mill and the Rock Springs logging site. The tram is taking a group of employees and families to the springs for a picnic c. 1907.

L.W. Gilliam, in the upper right corner, was postmaster for Clarcona from 1909 to 1916. Clark's Mill became the center of the settlement known as Clarcona. The post office is pictured above, in 1909, with unidentified people on porch.

Lilla Hammond married Lewis C. Osborn, who owned Lewis C. Osborn and Co., Ltd, dealers in general merchandise, at Zellwood, Florida, in 1911. She was the daughter of Willie and Mollie Hammond, who came to Apopka from Alabama in 1886.

Mayre Jackson visited his Apopka relative Irene Womble in 1911. In later years Mr. Jackson returned and recalled that some of his happiest days were spent in Apopka.

The State Bank of Apopka was organized in 1911. It survived the Depression and served the community for more than 50 years at three locations. The first bank in Apopka was established in 1885 with Edmond Prince as president. It closed in 1894 due to poor economy.

William G. Talton Sr. was a cashier of the State Bank of Apopka from 1911 to 1934. He became president after the death of William Edwards in 1934. When the Orange County Bankers Association was organized in 1934, William G. Talton Sr. was named its first president. He is pictured seated, in front of the vault, with O.E. McGuire and Frank Burgust standing.

Harry Ustler came to Florida in 1912 from Ohio. In the photo above John, Elwood, Harry, and Paul Ustler are clearing the land for the Ustler fernery

The Newell and Ustler Fernery is a picture of perfection with symmetrical slats and posts and lush ferns, the reward of good planning and hard work. This enterprise was credited with being the largest nursery in the south and was the source of Apopka's nickname, "The Fern City."

The Newell and Ustler Fernery was totally flattened by the cyclone of 1918.

The Apopka Union School, built in 1901, was totally destroyed during the cyclone of 1918, as were many homes and businesses. W.T. Champneys was sleeping on his couch when the storm struck. When the cyclone was over, Champneys was still on the couch, but he was out in the yard and not sleeping!

In 1913 Nellie Gilliam rides her horse from Clarcona to Lake Underhill in Orlando to visit her parents, Emma and Irving Reed. The Reeds came to Florida in 1904 from Dartmouth, Massachusetts.

Since Frank Davis was in the real estate business, it is not surprising that while he was an Apopkan councilman, he was also president of the town's improvement group. He married widow Abbie Waite, and the couple were renown for their community involvement.

Mildred A. Board chose this 1915 portrait to represent her family. She is shown with her father Lemuel, brother Leroy Brown, and mother Martha Ann Board. Mrs. Board was born in Apopka in her mother's home, which has been her lifelong home, on what is now West M.A. Board Street. Her life has been devoted to educating and mentoring Apopka children and teenagers. After 45 years in education, she retired in 1981.

John Grossenbacher, a plant pathologist, came to northwest Orange County on agriculture business in 1915 and stayed. He founded the Florida Insecticide Company, which manufactured and distributed insecticides for citrus application. He also published *The Citrus Leaf*, a monthly journal with a circulation of 5,000. His descendants continue to live in and serve the Apopka area.

This exciting picture records the engineering feat of raising the first power pole in Apopka, without mechanical equipment, to provide electricity. Electric lights were turned on in Apopka on February 10, 1915.

Adelbert Starbird kept stringing wires, providing power to the Consumers Lumber Company and Marshall Packing House in late 1915. In early 1916 he received authority from the county to erect lines along the highway to Plymouth and the Pirie Estate. Shown here on the Dixie Highway are A.M. Starbird, left, and George Walker, right.

The Apopka City Council authorized the Apopka Water, Light, and Ice Company in 1905 to use and occupy the streets to lay pipe for water and erect poles for wires over a period of 50 years. Adelbert M. Starbird, as manager of the utilities, was piping water to neighbors from his home well. There was a growing demand for water, so this wooden tower that stood 53 feet off the ground was built.

When Mallory Welch was eight years old he could not go to school until he was big enough to ride and care for his horse. This picture of Mallory on his horse, Billy, was taken years later. Mr. Welch was active in sports and was an outdoorsmen, serving as warden of Rock Springs Preserve in 1936. He grew Boston Ferns from 1922 to 1958. (Photo courtesy Mary Lee Welch.)

41

Apopka City Hall was built by Alfred Robbins and opened February 19, 1915. It was the site of a homecoming for veterans of World War I. This building was destroyed in 1926.

When the county declined to provide Apopka with a jail, the city contracted with W.L. Pannell to built one out of cement blocks, at a cost of about $300.00. It appears to be a single room structure with little ventilation. He also made the octagon-shaped stones for the sidewalks.

Carl Jackson was the franchised dealer for the Hanson Motor Company in Apopka. They were unable to develop a market for the cars and even though Jackson's garage was successful for six years, he sold it to R.A. Lasater and Dwight Risener. Above is a picture of George Hanson's living room and family.

Pictured is Miss Mattie Chapman driving her pupils to school in Apopka prior to 1920.

Harry Hewett lived on the southwest corner of Central and Myrtle Streets. He was an avid photographer and preserved the devastation of the cyclone of 1918 through his postcard photos. He enjoyed hunting and fishing, and he also kept bees and sold honey, sharing some with the bears. He is depicted showing one way to bring home the deer.

This hunter is certainly proud of his catch. No permit was required to hunt alligators.

Three

THE BOOM AND BUST ERA
1921–1935

As the "boom years" changed to the "gloom years" of the Depression, residents braced for the fall.

Nellie Burgust, Carmelita Wagner, Theo Whitted, and Frank Burgust are shown on their way to Apopka from St. Louis, Missouri, on October 29, 1921.

Nellie and Frank Burgust are going fishing with their cane poles at Lake Page, near Piedmont, in 1922.

Bennett Land Sr., an SALRR engineer, became associated with the mill early in the 1920s and in 1922 succeeded Austin Starbird as president of Consumers Lumber and Veneer. Bennett Land's sons, Bennett Jr., Henry, and John, were all involved in the mill. When Bennett Sr. died in 1935, Henry became president. The expanded mill is shown above years, c. 1939.

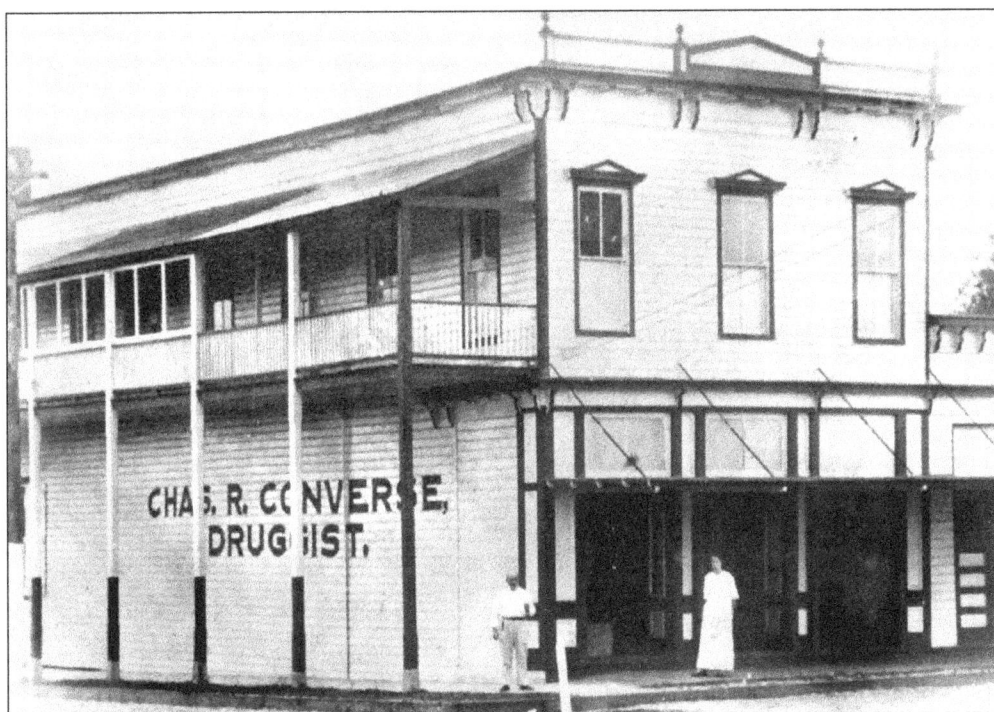

This drugstore was originally built by Dr. Charles R. Converse and was sold to Dr. Walter Sheppard in 1923. Sheppard's also had a soda counter and booths and served lunches to students and citizens, as well. After Dr. Sheppard died, his wife, Lillian Sheppard, an excellent business woman, managed the store. His three sons, Leon, Laurie, and Walter, became pharmacists and continued the pharmacy at the new location across the street until December 1, 1987.

Mrs. Carl (Nell) Jackson sold Fern City Sundries on the southwest corner of U.S. 441/Fourth Street and Central Avenue, to Elmer Rimel. The floors were ceramic tile, and the furniture was "ice cream parlor" metal chairs and tables. Popular frozen treats and sandwiches were served and newspapers and magazines were in abundance. People congregated to visit and share news. In later years this building housed Henri's Meat Market.

The Apopka High School was built in the early 1920s. It is presently the Apopka City Hall.

The William Edwards Hotel, built in the 1920s, was later known as the Palms Hotel. It was later replaced by the First Federal Building.

The Apopka United Daughters of the Confederacy chapter was formed in 1921 by Florence Collier. It is one of the longest continuously running organizations in the city. The original chapter house was sold and the proceeds were put in a trust to provide scholarships for deserving students. The money has helped many students with educational expenses.

The Apopka Baseball team of 1926 is, from left to right, (front row) Mallory Welch, Leland Hawthorne, Oscar Cashwell, Robert Rencher, and Leon Sheppard; (middle row) V.A. Stewart, Winifred Harris, Percy Starbird Jr., unidentified, and R.G. Pitman; (back row) Carl Jackson, Larry Lasater, Tobe Edwards, Paul Ustler, and Ira Erickson. The boy in front is unidentified. During the 1920s Mallory Welch, Walter Schopke, Larry Lasater, and Winifred Harris rotated in the positions of manager and captain.

Dr. Howard Kelly of Camden, New Jersey, gave the area known as Rock Springs to Orange County in 1927 for a recreation area. In pre–Civil War days it was a plantation owned by William Delk. Dr. Kelly was an eminent surgeon and pioneer in the use of radium in the treatment of cancer. He was also a powerful lay speaker for the Methodist church.

Centered among her students in 1928 is Mrs. Kitty Stewart, a good teacher and stern disciplinarian. She taught hundreds of Apopka students; played the piano for schools, weddings, funerals, and Methodist church services; and led a Brownie troop. She and Mr. V.A. Stewart were great dancers. Every child's name is listed on the back of the picture. Come to the museum to identify them!

This group of ladies enjoy an afternoon of bridge, c. 1930. Pictured are, from left to right, (front row) Blanche Edwards, Elizabeth Welch, and Jennie V. Harris; (back row) Marie Pryce, Ethel Jackson, Nell Jackson, and Mary Walters. (Courtesy of W.W. Walters.)

The Apopka High School football team of 1934 played great football and also developed into great leaders for our community.

Jean, Robert, and Ruth Burgust are pictured with Poochie and Mickey, the chicken, about 1935. The girls' costumes were made of crepe paper for school plays. The dresses were inexpensive to make but scratchy and none too durable or waterproof.

Cooper's Grocery was located at the corner of U.S. 441 and Bradshaw, with Old Dixie Highway behind the store. John H. Cooper owned and operated this early convenience store that served the northwest side of town. (Courtesy of Wanda Blackmon.)

The new city hall was built in 1935 with WPA workers providing much of the labor. It served as the city office, tag office, and theater, with the police department and jail housed in the back. This picture was taken later, as it shows the new State Bank of Apopka.

Four

OUT OF DEPRESSION
AND INTO WAR
1936–1950

Collecting scrap metal, walking instead of riding, and adjusting to rationing were ways to support the war effort. Four local servicemen gave their lives for our freedom: Harold Caldwell, Jack Grossenbacher, Albert Martin Jr., and Dick Wells. Six young men interrupted their education but returned to graduate in 1946: J.D. Carleton, Billy Cox, Dale Cross, Louis Strickland, Jack Urquhart, and J.D. Odom. Merton Raulerson graduated later.

Thomas Swanner moved to Apopka in 1927 and bought the Wayside Inn in 1936. He was a city judge for 18 years, executive vice president of the State Bank of Apopka for 45 years, member of the Apopka Rotary Club, and a Master Mason. He served as justice of the peace for four years. Mr. and Mrs. Swanner lived on Park Avenue for many years. In later years he lived on Magnolia Street.

Lake Apopka was noted for its big-mouth bass. Fishing lured tourists to Apopka and to "Fisherman's Paradise," shown above; Johnson's Fishing Camp; and Lovell's Landing.

Miss Orlin Mitchell, seen here with her first grade class, is remembered as a compassionate teacher, dispensing discipline with love.

Allen Chisholm was a fresh produce businessman in northwest Orange County for more than 60 years. He had no mode of transportation in the beginning. He took orders for produce, placed them in large tan-colored woven baskets, and walked to customers' homes. As his business grew, he purchased a Model A Ford truck for home deliveries. He was a welcome sight, especially to people who had no transportation.

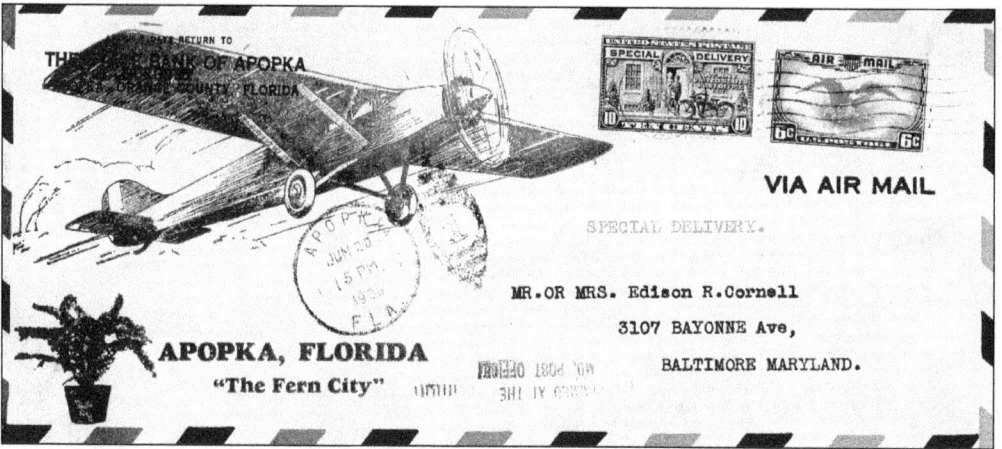

The State Bank of Apopka utilized lightweight airmail envelopes that advertised "The Fern City." This one was postmarked June 20, 1938. (Courtesy of J. Juckette.)

Lenora Gilliam Rimel and her brother, Cpl. Delbert Gilliam, who was serving with the 397th Bombardment Squadron in World War II, enjoy time together.

Howard Goolsby and Annie Mae
Kirkland pose at the Consumers
Lumber and Veneer Company site
on Eighth Street prior to his leaving
to serve in World War II. They were
married after he returned to Apopka.

Little Ken Gilliam poses respectfully in
his sailor suit with daddy, Leroy Gilliam,
about 1945.

Raymond Anderson Sr. served his country in World War II.

T.Sgt. Estus Rawls is pictured in his World War II uniform in the 1940s. The reason he is smiling is that he didn't even smoke; the cigarette was the cameraman's idea. (Courtesy of Ron Rawls.)

Sgt. William J. Bogar was stationed in Sardinia in 1944 or 1945 while serving his country.

Garrett I. Gilliam served in World War II and returned to serve the citizens by providing grove caretaking to owners who lived away or needed that service. He was also a Mason.

61

Making the best of Christmas away from home is a group stationed at Membury Field in England in December 1944. Bennie Driggers is the third from the left on the back row.

Gene Christmas, home on leave, is pictured with Belle Gilliam, c. 1944. The picture was taken at the Dixie Service Station.

Grateful appreciation and pride fills our hearts as we remember what this picture represents. Skill, training, dedication, and courage are shown in this 455th Bomber Group of the 741st Bomb Squadron photo. Second Lt. Winfield Bowers Jr. is third from the left on the back row.

During the war ladies from our community served in the Red Cross by rolling bandages, making slings, sending packages to service men, and helping in our hometown. Most of these ladies are unidentified except Myrtle Rogers, who is third from the left in the front row, and Nellie Burgust, fourth from the left in back.

Win Bowers served in the 15th Air Force in the Italy Campaign. He flew B-24 planes. He and his wife, Dorothy, own and operate the Sky Bolt Aeronautical Corporation, established in 1981.

As the war raged overseas, peacekeeping efforts continued at home with Fred L. Risener as chief of police, with no two way radios, scanners, or a city-owned vehicle. Gas was rationed even for him. He implemented the use of finger printing in Apopka in those early days.

This 1945 pyramid of power gave courage to the home team. Shown here, from top to bottom and left to right, are Ovida Dickey, Viola Kerr, Jane Hall, Winifred Harris, Mary Land, Betty Hall, Ruth Reiners, and Martha Haynes.

The Midget Grill, at Highland Avenue and Fourth Street, served as the "gathering place" for teenagers during the 1940s and 1950s. Meeting, eating hamburgers and hot dogs, and dancing on the pavilion in the rear served as the only "recreational" facility in town.

This 1944 photograph shows members on the steps of Apopka Methodist Church at the corner of Third Street and Park Avenue.

Dan Vaden and Lorena Smith display their string of fish caught at Lake Apopka in February 1946.

This 1946 hunting party at Joe Carroll's camp at the Apopka Sportsman's Club includes (from left to right) three unidentified men; Joe Carroll; and Ken, Arlie, Roy, Garrett, and Jack Gilliam.

Otis Chance founded the Mt. Sinai Seventh Day Adventist Church in Apopka. He is shown here with his wife Johnnie Mae, who came to Apopka with her parents, Joseph and Sarah Jones, when she was 11 years old. (Courtesy of Aaron Chance.)

VOMAC GROVES U.S. #441, PLYMOUTH, FLORIDA
Grower and Shipper of Florida Citrus. Sun Ripened Fruit Direct to You.

Roadside fruit stands were popular stops for tourists during the height of Central Florida's citrus seasons. Fred Macwithey owned the Vo-Mac site in Plymouth. His daughter, Susan McCarthy, has written a book entitled *Lay That Trumpet in Our Hands*, depicting her father's memories of Civil Rights activities in the area in the 1950s and early 1960s.

Five

MATURING MILESTONES 1951–1965

The first telephone office building in Apopka also housed the chief telephone operator and her family. What advances we were to experience in the coming years in technology!

Principal Roger A. Williams is flanked by faculty members of grades 1 through 12 in 1951. Later students in grades 1 through 6 were transferred to Dream Lake, Lovell, or Apopka Elementary

Thomas B. King's Electrical and Plumbing store in 1950 was located on Central Avenue near U.S. 441. Dale Hall's barber shop is shown on the right side of this picture.

72

Schools, and the building was then put to use by the Apopka Fire Department. The building housing grades 7 through 12 is now Apopka City Hall.

The current First United Methodist Church, at the corner of Park Avenue and Second Street, was completed in 1951.

It took great effort to avoid power lines and safely add the steeple to the new Presbyterian church, built in 1952. The church is located at 500 S. Highlands Street.

The Tinsley House provided room and board for many residents as well as travelers. The Rotary Club met here on Thursdays and anyone could come for lunch in an attractive dining room with cloth table covers and napkins. It was located on the north side of U.S. 441/Fourth Street.

Blackwelder's Dept. Store was a favorite spot for shoppers, offering both fashionable and functional items. This was formerly Gilliard's Family Store with the Gilliard family living in the back of the store.

This photo shows West Fruit Company, which existed under other names over time. It was the Richardson Packing House and the Apopka Fruit Company as well as West Fruit Company. On the left is the Seaboard Railway Station. The road enters from S. Central Avenue.

Lela Lovell, Eastern Star Worthy Grand Matron, and officers were installed in 1953 at the Masonic Lodge.

Choir members provide inspirational songs for service in the new First Presbyterian Church. Pews were not yet available so the seats from the demolished theater were used temporarily.

This image of U.S. 441/Fourth Street provides a view of Apopka prior to 1955, from west to east at the Central Avenue intersection. The Palms Hotel is on the left and O.E. McGuire's Standard Oil Station is on the right.

Dream Lake Elementary School's faculty is shown with Howard Beckert, principal. In 1955 this 15-classroom school was erected on the old airport property. Beckert recalls battling mounds of sand, which had to be shoveled off sidewalks prior to landscaping. He also recalls rising early to restart the boiler on cold mornings. Students from the downtown school were transferred to Dream Lake, Lovell, or Apopka Elementary Schools.

The King's Auto Parts building served Apopkans for years, also under the names of Tower Hardware in 1919, as John Jackson/R.G. Widrig's Hardware, and as William and Dave Edwards and Carl Jackson's Hardware in 1922. John Jackson continued to operate the Service Garage. Apartments were for rent upstairs. The local bus stopped there for passengers. The Greyhound Bus Station was across the street facing U.S. 441. This photo was taken January 12, 1958.

Mr. W.G. Talton Sr. accepts his mail from Bud Robinson, carrier, while Robert Burgust looks on.

Central Ave, Apopka, Florida

Tom Swanner

Perry Warren

Garrett Gilliam

Sonny Thompson

Garrett Gilliam and Sonny Thompson lead the parade's horses onto Fifth Street from Central Avenue. Perry Warren and Tom Swanner follow as they celebrate the 100th anniversary of the Masonic Lodge in 1956.

Six

BUSINESS AND
BOUNDARY GROWTH
1966–1980

Business and boundary growth was in all directions from City Hall, Errol Estates, Zellwood Station, and Disney attractions. Subdivisions and shopping centers seemed to spring up overnight.

With thousands of acres of orange groves surrounding Apopka, it is not surprising that the Citrus Growers Association was at one time the largest employer in the area.

Smiles all around as G. Kirk Lewis, Sally Millitzer, Don Evans, and Mayor Land receive the President's Award at the Central Florida Fair in 1965. The "Town of Apopka City, Florida" sign is now housed in the museum.

The Apopka High School Class of 1945 gathers for a 20-year reunion.

Celebrating the Apopka Women's Club's 10th anniversary in 1967, we have six past presidents: Mary Stewart, Alice Beth Miner, Kit Nelson, Mary Lee Welch, Irene Ustler, and Esther Brosche. This is Apopka's most active club, with their main activities being the Art and Foliage Festival held each spring and the Miss Apopka Pageant, the latter being affiliated with the Miss America Pageant.

Seen here meeting at the State Capitol are Miss Apopka Nancy Carol McClure, Burnie Roberts, Fran Carlton, Gov. Bob Graham, Eltha Mark (president of Apopka Women's Club), Joan Alsup, and Stella Swanberg.

In 1968 a very important event took place when ground was broken for the North Orange Memorial Hospital. Florida Hospital Apopka, as it is now known, continually grows and receives upgrades, bringing the most modern equipment for diagnosing and treating patients to Apopka.

Dr. T.E. McBride, Mayor John Land, Congressman Ed Gurney, and John Talton attend the hospital's ribbon cutting ceremony.

(above left) Dr. "Tommy" McBride, left, was part of the hospital staff, and he served Apopkans for many decades, once declaring "3,000 babies and still counting." It is said that had he collected all the monies owed him, his house, which is now Townsends Restaurant, could have been lined with gold.

(above right) In 1970 Dr. Tommy's son Robin, right, opened up his practice in the city and continued attending to patients for over 20 years. He actually treated Apopkans who had watched him grow up.

These hospital staff members, photographed in 1969, include Nellie Rolfe, Les Palmer, Daisy Smith, Betty Wilson, Margaret Cox, Priscilla Young, Eveline Mihalko, Mary Bronson, Mary Wheeler, Bernice DeRyke, and Frank Meyer.

Get-togethers are
popular in our city.
Taken in the 1970s, this
photo shows a group
of Apopkans getting
together for an "old-
timers" luncheon.

Sheppard's Drugstore was a local landmark for many years—a gathering place to keep up with all of the local gossip.

In the 1970s, when Disney opened in Kissimmee, great changes began to take place in Apopka. Bill Bradshaw conducts the Apopka High School Band at the opening ceremonies of Disney World's Magic Kingdom.

With all of the ensuing activity in the Central Florida area, new businesses began to flourish, and at Sheeler and U.S. 441, Apopka saw its first shopping center.

A large variety of plants were grown in Apopka nurseries, and an addition in 1971 was Engelmann Nursery, with around 10 employees. Today that number has increased to 200. Father and son Herman and Wolfgang Engelmann have always been a vital part of the community, opening their nursery to bus tours and generously donating to local events.

As the area changed, the beautiful orange groves began to disappear to make way for subdivisions.

Richard Mark started Errol Estate subdivision with its 27 holes of golf situated on the old Pirie Estate. Permanent residents and snowbirds alike came to find their place in the sun. Sandhill Cranes, birds of a different kind, also choose to live here in Errol Estate.

In 1971 Sisters Ann and Teresa, desiring to help migrant workers, assisted in forming the Farmworkers Ministry and later the West Orange Health Center, which is known today as the Community Health Center. They also started an adult literacy program and many programs for children.

Getting ready for the Big Potato Slow Pitch Softball Tournament of 1975 is Big Potato, himself, being crowned by Betty Daniels, city recreational director.

Sports have always been a large part of life for Apopkans, and in 1973 this ambitious team of Mary Fly, Jeannette Robinson, Bud Robinson, Joe Stephens, Henry Land, Martha Henry, Agnes Smith, Dr. Tommy McBride, Florence Sheppard, and John Land line up for a tournament. Do they perhaps have Wimbledon in mind?

Apopka's basketball team of 1975 appears to be trying to outdo a Michael Jordan jump.

Apopka Foliage Sertoma Club was formed in 1974. Shown here in a recent photo, from left to right, are "Mac" McGuffin, "Coz" Mizell, Tom Collins, Mayor John Land, and Bob Smith, five current Sertomans who were among the founding members. "Sertoma" is a contraction of SERVICE TO MANKIND, and the national organization's focus is raising money to assist deaf children. The club participates in many community activities, including the Christmas Parade and the popular Little Miss and Cutie Pie pageants.

In 1976 the Apopka Foliage Sertoma Club took over the Christmas Parade from the chamber of commerce. The club, with the City, organizes this event, and it has grown to some 90 participants with thousands lining our streets to enjoy this annual spectacle.

In 1980 a group of residents of Zellwood Station decided to form a service group; thus was born "Zellwood Station Redcaps." Through the years they have served the community in many

ways. Their annual golf tournament has raised thousands of dollars for Apopka Hospital. Food programs are helped, toys are made, and many children are mentored by this untiring group.

Another very active Apopkan civic organization is the Rotary Club. Photographed here are, from left to right (front row) Bob Burgust, Willis Warren, Bob Pitman, Mayor John Land, Henry Land, Dr. Henry Ansley, Bill Morris, and Lowell Swanberg; (back row) David Black, David Rankin, Jim Wade, Giles VanDuyne, John Ricketson, Christ Hart, Bill Arrowsmith, Steve Preston, and Charlie Hughes.

Apopka's Deanna Pitman, Miss Florida, is pictured with Mayor Land, former Miss America Vonda Kay Von Dyke, AWC President Kay Huth, and Joan Alsup, A.W.C.'s Miss Apopka liaison.

Seven

MARCHING TO THE MILLENNIUM 1981–2000

The ROTC cadets stride out to 2000.

Getting in the spirit of our Centennial Celebration in 1982 are city clerk Bonnie Bray, commissioners Dick Mark and Alonzo Williams, Mayor John Land, commissioners Bill Arrowsmith and Detmer Rouzer, and mayor's secretary Sharon Mills.

Not to be outdone by the others, Johnie McLeod stands prepared for the Civil War re-enactment.

Apopka Women's Club president Eltha Mark receives the keys to the city from Mayor Land as they stand before the beautiful metal fern presented to the city by the Women's Club in acknowledgment that Apopka was once known as "Fern City."

The Catfish Place is a favorite eating place for locals. In 1982 Bob and Elaine Johnson took over the 1928 building and made this a regular "must" for the entire area. Always willing to help out a good cause, they are as famous for their good works as they are for their good food.

In 1985 Richard Anderson became fire chief and under his direction the department has grown and is recognized as one of the finest fire stations in Central Florida. Chief Anderson assists former fire chief Norman Ustler in unveiling a plaque to commemorate Norman Ustler's service to Apopka as Norman's family look on.

Is this a little lip service here?

Belle and Boo Gilliam are shown inside their new fern greenhouse, which opened in early 1985. Although Apopka is no longer known as "Fern City" many ferneries still exist.

Nelson roses are now nationally known. In the 1960s brothers B.P. and Earl Nelson started cultivating their now-famous roses, and here the brothers and their families stand amidst the beautiful flowers.

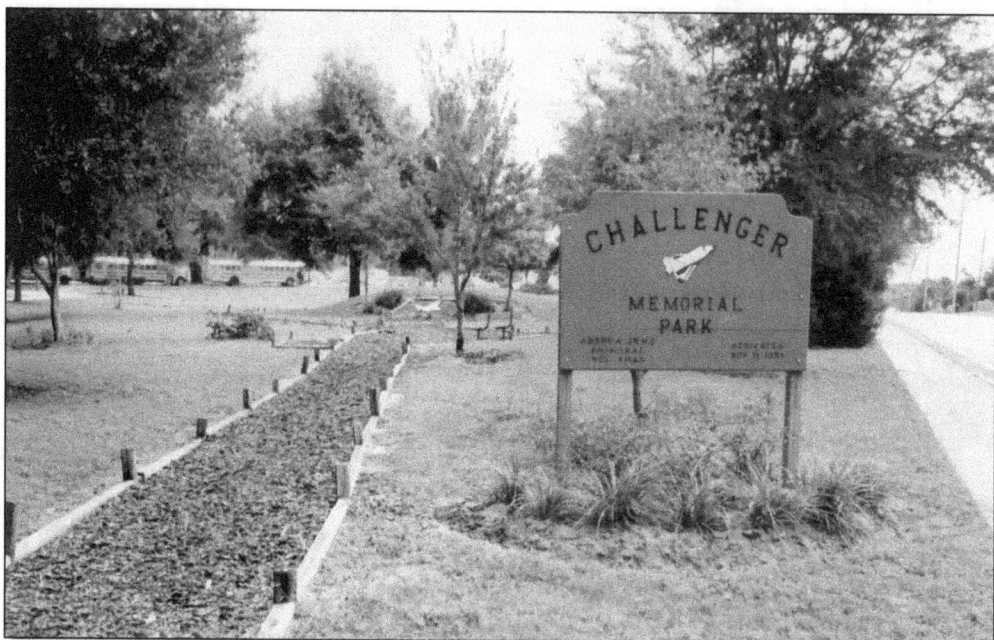

In 1986 the Challenger tragedy, felt throughout our nation, stirred the students of Apopka Middle School to organize a fund-raiser for this permanent memorial at the corner of Votaw and Park.

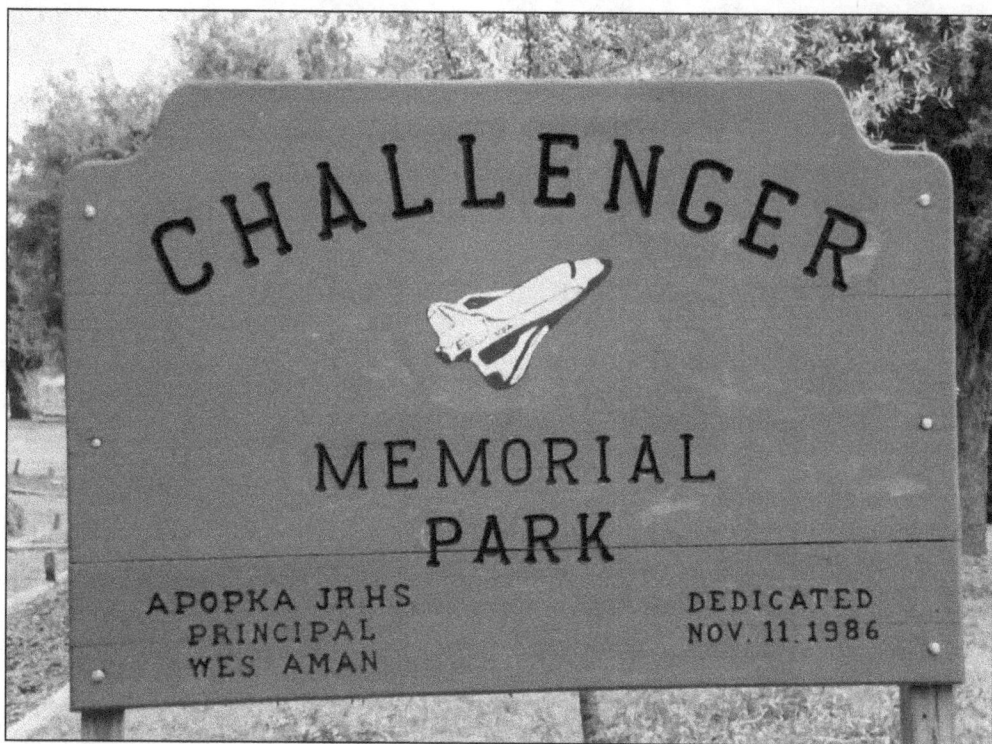

The memorial is set at the corner of Park and Votaw.

The First Baptist Church has seen many alterations, and this modern structure at the corner of U.S. 441 and Highland stands as a monument to its faithful members.

The Apopka Assembly of God's beautiful building is located on Park Street. The first services were held there in 1988. The church has been part of Apopka for several decades and was originally located on U.S. 441 and Bradshaw. Under the leadership of Pastor Kevin Craig the church has seen its congregation grow, and it has introduced many diverse programs.

Pastor Williams leads the Pentecostal Church on U.S. 441. This handsome building was completed in 1988, and the church has experienced phenomenal growth in its attendance and its many varied activities.

Pictured is the joyful choir of the Pentecostal Church.

The First United Methodist women gather for a photo session at their fellowship supper, when a delicious meal is cooked and served by the Methodist men's group and is followed by very entertaining entertainment! (Courtesy of S. Johnson.)

The Methodist men's group, known throughout the church for their culinary skills, appear to have finished all their kitchen duties. (Courtesy of S. Johnson.)

Apopka's chief of police Tom Collins and his famous automobile were a familiar sight from 1971 to 1991. Although he retired from the force in 1991 he continues to serve the community through involvement in many local activities.

Joseph Brown became Apopka's new chief of police in 1995. He is seen here with his group of officers. Under his direction the force has grown and can boast that it has some of the most up-to-date electronic equipment available for modern-day law enforcement.

Apopka's recreational department, involved in so many community activities, was in dire need of new facilities, and in 1990 the Fran Carlton Community Center opened. The department oversees many programs, such as summer camp, arts and crafts classes, dancing, bridge, and exercise classes, as well as arranging trips to outlying points of interest for seniors.

Getting ready for an AARP meeting at the center, from left to right, are Tom Collins, seated; Mae Chustz, who served the city untiringly in a variety of ways; and Dottie Kolkmeyer. Many families and organizations rent space at the center for their private functions.

From left to right in this photo of the Sportsmen's Club are Bill Hogshead, R.B. "Bunny" Hogshead, Bennett Land, Tom Mahaffey, Henry Land, John Land, and George McClure.

Dr. Joseph L. Akerman provided medical care to many Apopkans from 1953 to 1989. He worked tirelessly with the Boy Scouts of America and was active in the First Presbyterian Church and the Breakfast Sertoma Club. He and his wife Orfa had five children and were involved in many local school activities.

William G. Talton Jr., born and raised in Apopka, worked in real estate and served in the First Baptist Church. He demonstrated the qualities of a true Christian by visiting the shut-ins and sharing the word of the Gospels.

The delighted occupants, the Sharonda Bradford family, stand outside their new home, which in 1992 was the first house built in Apopka by Habitat for Humanity.

High School reunions are popular, and here we have Apopka High School alumni covering

several years.

Love of Apopka and Country is evident by the support given to local servicemen's clubs. Here members of VFW Post 10147 gather to prepare for a visit to the Veterans' Hospital in Gainesville. They organize many fund-raising events, enabling them to take supplies to our hospitalized veterans. Their poppy-selling effort is extended throughout our area.

On Veterans Day, Apopkans, led by VFW members, attend the solemn ceremony of placing a wreath at the war memorial in Greenwood Cemetery. This monument honors service personnel who served in all wars, including Korea and Vietnam.

The beautiful Champney House was transported through Apopka to a new site on Welch Road to make room for commercial buildings.

Businesses came with rapid succession on U.S. 441/Main Street. Nationally known pharmacies have been a part of Apopka for many years, and in 2000 Walgreens opened their new "free-standing" store on the site of the Champney House.

Mayor Land stands with Apopka's representative Andy Gardner, our Little League champions, and their coaches. Long shall we remember the fame this national winning team brought to Apopka.

This beautiful home was originally built on Highlands Street for the Eldredge family. Later bought by Dr. T.E. McBride, it is now known as Townsend's Plantation.

Eight

APOPKA MUSEUM MENTORS

The earliest museum mentors were our ancestors who saved and protected bits and pieces of treasured memories so they would not be forgotten. The motto "The Past is my Heritage, the Present is my Responsibility, and the Future is my Challenge" clearly places the focus on the museum's purpose. As all good things eventually come to an end, so must Apopka's journey. This chapter concludes our journey into the past with snapshots that illustrate better than words how events and people have supported the growth and development of the Museum of Apopkans.

In 1971 the public was invited to visit the first museum in the Apopka City Hall. The officers consisted of Elizabeth Grossenbacher (shown at left), president; John H. Land, vice president; Reba Evans, treasurer and recording secretary; Mary Lee Welch, corresponding secretary; Edward A. Miner, curator; and Harry P. Witherington, librarian, with Mildred Whiteside and Kathleen Stewart completing the board of directors' roster. The museum's second home was in the former medical office of Dr. "Tommy" McBride. Finally, the City of Apopka provided office space on Fifth Street until the completion of the new permanent Museum of Apopkans next door.

Initially the community was blessed by a few citizens who realized the past would play a significant role in its future. Emily Jackson Swanson was among those who staunchly believed in the preservation of historical mementos. An active participant in 1968, when the Apopka Historical Society, Inc. came into being, she continued to work for the museum for the rest of her life.

In the foreground, Orlin Mitchell Healy, Kathleen Stewart, and Ruby Haygood are among those attending the first open house.

Mrs. Josephine Land was a charter member and a board director of the Museum of Apopkans who devoted many hours to the museum and to her beloved First Presbyterian Church, where, for many years, she served as treasurer. During World War II, four of her sons served their country. "Miss Jo" also has the distinction of being the mother of Apopka's 50-year-term mayor.

Mary Lee Welch and Emma Alcorn tend the museum booth at the chamber of commerce's Business Connection Exhibit. The booth displayed relics of the past.

Brewster Bray, Janet Connelly, Pauline Stokes, and Bennett Land admire the Native American artifacts.

Pauline Stokes, Kit Land Nelson, Belle Gilliam, and Sue Simpson, along with Bennett Land and Janet Connelly in the back, were some of the museum's ardent supporters.

Mrs. Gladden, loved and honored by students of Phyllis Wheatley, advised her 1962 graduates: "Be not content with the little glory which is yours today, but continue upward on the ladder until you reach the height where you, too, will be one in the grand view of the far horizon. There you will join with those who are dedicated to the task of making our world a better place in which to live."

Just picture a person who has touched many lives through her teaching by being one of the founders of the Apopka Historical Society, by serving a term as president, and by continuing to serve as a director of the executive board. Add to this mix the editing of the museum's newsletter and the writing of a weekly column, condense all facets into "community spirit," and there you have the person—Janet Connelly.

The Miner family played a major role in the development of the Piedmont area. The leadership continues today with Norris and Alice Beth Miner, both of whom have given countless hours to the community and to the museum, serving as board members, docents, and volunteers for outside functions such as visiting schools and manning booths.

At the Mother's Day Tea, waitresses Bettie Hicks and Mary Elizabeth Wheeler take a break to visit with Katherine Hinton and vice president Angela Nichols.

Kay Hethcox, a devoted member, has worked many hours for the museum and is seen here with Ed Hlinak studying the artifacts that have been donated.

John Ricketson, publisher of the *Apopka Chief* and *Planter* newspapers, always has a smile and a friendly response for pleas of help for advertisements, research, pictures, or whatever the request. Thanks, John.

On the steps of our beautiful city hall we have the mayor (front row, center) and our city leaders. From left to right, they are (front row) Mark Holmes, Janice Goebel, and Bill Arrowsmith; (back row) Billy Dean, Richard Anderson, Jack Douglas, and Marilyn McQueen.

No journey is possible without leadership, from our determined forefathers to the present. Dignitaries from far and wide, along with hometown folks, joined in the Apopka Area Chamber of Commerce's celebration of Mayor John H. Land's 50 years in office.

Mayor John Land and wife, Betty, are shown with their children, Sue, on his left, and Cathy and Johnny in front.

Richard Anderson has served as president and in other capacities on the board of the museum. Through his efforts and with help from members of the fire department and the city building department, who volunteered many hours of their off-duty time, our Log Cabin Museum became a reality.

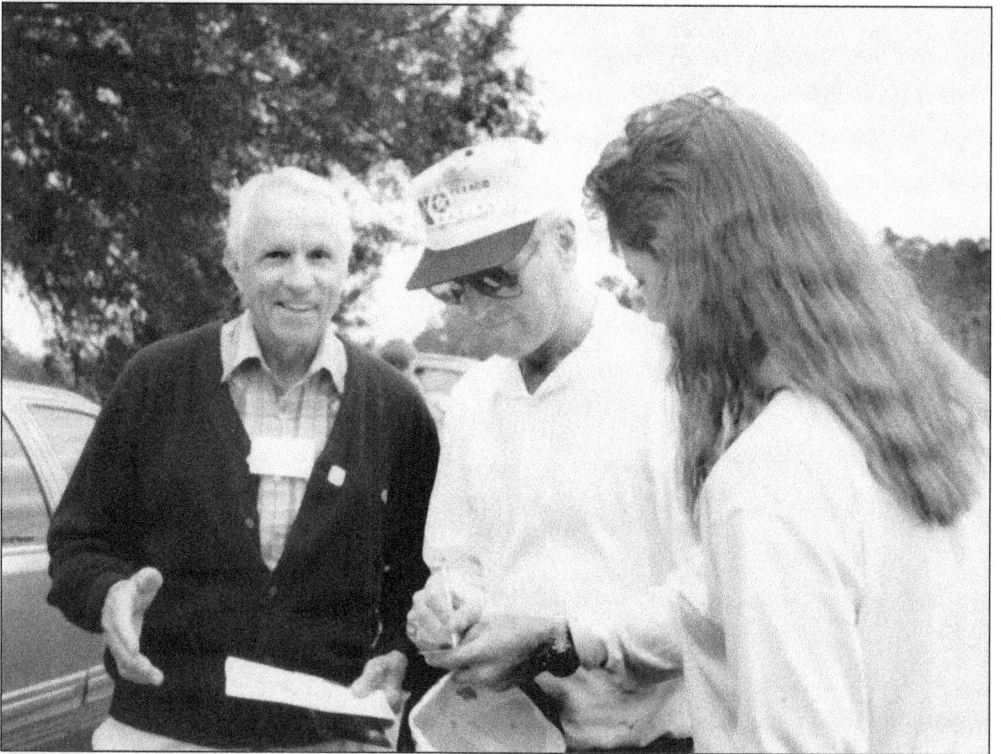

Even Paul Newman takes time out to sign an autograph for "Hiz'onor."

126

At age 21, upon his father's death, Henry Land became president of Consumers Lumber and Veneer Co. He had the distinction of being the youngest Orange County Commissioner before resigning to serve in World War II. In 1952, he became a representative in the Florida State Legislature. In 1975, he was instrumental in the sale of North Orange Memorial Hospital to Florida Hospital; revenues from that sale enable medical scholarships for qualifying students.

Mayor Land proudly addresses the crowd at the grand opening of the museum's new building, just as he stands proud in the growth of his hometown, now the second largest city in Orange County. Hail to the Chief!

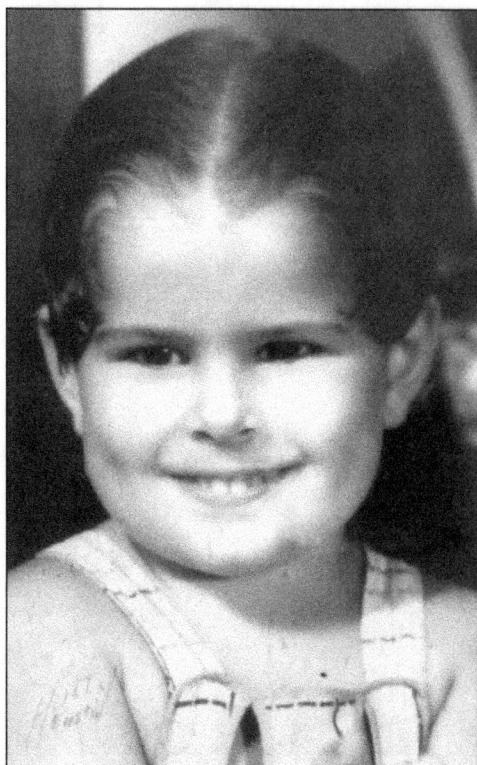

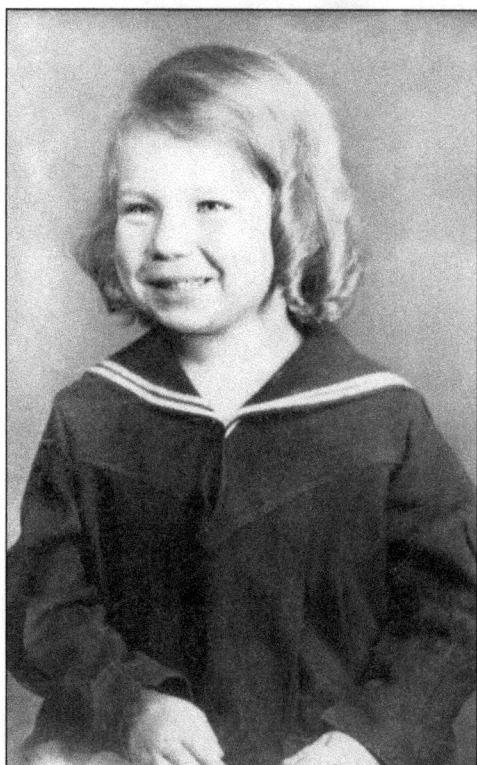

Three babes, here we sit,
never thought a book we'd writ
Now it's done with loving care,
with our community we gladly share.

www.ingramcontent.com/pod-product-compliance
Lightning Source LLC
Chambersburg PA
CBHW080549110426
42813CB00006B/1256